21
INSIGHTS
I WISH MOM
TAUGHT ME

GAIL MARIE KING

*This book is dedicated to my
Lord Jesus Christ, to my family,
and to every wonderful person
I've been blessed to know!*

Contents

21
INSIGHTS
I WISH MOM
TAUGHT ME

INTRODUCTION

I have been truly fortunate to meet really incredible people. It occurred to me that sharing the knowledge we've acquired through life experiences is one of the most significant things we can offer. As a woman, mother, entrepreneur, and child of God, my experiences have been extensive. However, I don't purport to know it all. The focus of this book is to share a few of the *most valuable* insights I've gained in life.

It's ironic that we often don't fully comprehend the importance of wisdom until we reach our 50s and beyond. And while many of the points may *appear* basic, they are essential to living a successful life. In our youth we may underestimate their significance. I am regularly startled concerning the insufficient preparation our homes and schools are providing for young adults. Our children are not spiritually, emotionally, or financially equipped to navigate a balanced, successful, and productive life.

I pray that what I share will resonate with the goodness that's already present in your heart. As a parent, I've grown to appreciate how much each new generation depends on the wisdom, counsel, and example of previous generations.

Despite being a single mother, my mom (who has passed away) did a phenomenal job supporting five children. She tried her best. This book examines twenty-one insights that I wished I'd known earlier in life.

However, what mom *did* share with me included the following.

- She shared her faith in God. That was priceless!

- I learned parenting from her unconditional love for all five of her children. She never gave up on any of us.

- She taught me that family loyalty is foundational and forever.

- Her example impressed upon me the rewards of hard work and perseverance. She was determined to master higher education and excel in the workplace. She believed that college was a ticket to a better life. She was right.

- She modeled creativity as she improvised and improved what we had.

- Her generosity and compassion were unforgettable.

- Mom was from Little Rock, Arkansas. Through her life, I grew to greatly respect people from the South. Their years of manual labor molded them into many of America's most successful leaders because their work ethic is exceptional.

- Mom shared her "down-home" appreciation for greens, beans, and smothered white potatoes with grilled onions.

- In society, she advised me to stand up for myself and avoid being gullible. Instead, I must challenge stereotypes, do my own research, and ask the tough questions.

- I admired her strength of character, her unrelenting spirit, and her physical strength.

- Her genuine love for all people was infectious.

- She was a good listener, humorous, and generously shared both her hardships and sage advice. Mom was genuinely unpretentious, pleasant, and hospitable.

- True to her nurturing demeanor, she loved our pets and treated them like family. Outdoors, she doted on her flowers and filled our yard with the most magnificent roses we could imagine.

It was a challenge for my mother to assume the role of mom *and dad* to three sons and two daughters. While mom focused on providing basic necessities like food, shelter, and safety, she had little time to contemplate *the purpose of life.*

I applaud her hard work and sacrifice and miss her dearly.

However, in the last few decades, I have come to realize that our children need much more than food and shelter. Merely keeping their physical bodies alive is insufficient. If we overlook the nourishment of their spirit and soul, they can live very shallow and even *tragic* lives.

My mom has passed on, but her legacy of love, strength, and ingenuity lives on.

The most valuable gift she left me was her faith in God.

The insights mentioned here are thought-provoking. I wish mom and I had more time to explore them. Nonetheless, in her honor, let's clarify and confirm the wisdom I've gleaned from decades of living and from her amazing example.

With love, I offer the following insights, hoping that they will encourage you to aim for your highest aspirations.

21 Insights

I WISH MOM
TAUGHT ME

One

OUR MOST IMPORTANT POSSESSION IN LIFE IS OUR RELATIONSHIP WITH GOD.

*B*lessed is the man who has a close relationship with God *early in life.* I believe that if I'd developed my faith earlier, God's wisdom would have prevented me from making foolish mistakes. Most of us are taught to do well in school and in business.

> **However only a handful of parents realize their first assignment is to make sure their child has her own relationship with God.**

When our children know God intimately and can hear Him clearly, parents are less inclined to worry about them. As a result of having a solid moral foundation and value system, our children can have more positive outcomes in terms of achievement and emotional well-being.

Even if our parents didn't take God seriously, we can. In fact, when we do, it will have a positive effect on the lives of our parents and every person we interact with.

Develop a close personal relationship with God, as early in life as possible. Never allow Satan to tell you that you aren't good enough – that's a lie. Right now, God yearns to tell you how much He loves you and wants to help you!

The fear of the LORD is the beginning
of wisdom; all who follow his precepts have
good understanding. To him belongs eternal
praise (Psalm 111:10, NIV).

Two

FEELING OVERWHELMED?

Take time off. Pray. Seek godly counsel. Remember that not all advice is good, so be very careful who (and what) you listen to. At times, for clarity, we must step away from challenges to pray and get a sound night's sleep.

Right now, (inside) we have *everything* we need to succeed in life. We strive to do our best with the resources available to us, and we never allow our limitations to hinder our progress. Be strong and courageous.

> **Resist anger and unforgiveness, as they cause us to make bad choices and say things we regret later.**

I promise you, as we begin to ask God for answers through prayer, He will direct and defend us.

Trust in the LORD with all your heart;
do not depend on your own understanding.
Seek his will in all you do, and he will show you
which path to take (Proverbs 3:5-6, NLT).

Three

PRIORITIZE WITH WISDOM.

God (our Creator) deserves to be first in our lives; next is family, and last is our career (or ministry). Jobs, houses, cars, money, and some friends will come and go. And we won't take them with us when we die.

Why do so many people neglect God while they are young and strong?

Is it because we feel invincible, indestructible, and as if we don't need Him? Or is it because we don't want to hear what He has to say? Do we fear that God's Word could get in the way of our having fun? Regardless of the excuse, it's a huge mistake to ignore our spiritual life.

> **The Lord is our primary and most reliable source of wisdom, comfort, provision, and protection.**

God is *never* mad at us. The Lord is waiting patiently for us to get to know Him. At the end of our life, we will want to know God and be lovingly connected with family and friends. In that day, we will not wish we had spent more time working to earn additional money.

Value relationships above material possessions. This is especially true concerning our own family. We can't despise anyone in our family; instead, we should think of ways to help them.

> **We have no obligation to be anyone's victim, but in the very least, we can pray for them.**

But seek first the kingdom of God and His righteousness, and all these things shall be added to you (Matthew 6:33, NKJV).

Four

STUDY THE WORD OF GOD.

*O*MG, this is huge! I truly wish I had been taught the Bible (in our home) during my youth.

The Holy Bible is a book of pure wisdom.

The Bible contains 66 books and letters by numerous authors over a span of hundreds of years. According to Guinness World Records, the best-selling book of all time is the Christian Bible. An estimated 5 billion copies have been sold and distributed.

There is a very practical reason for the phenomenal success and longevity of the Holy Bible. The Bible truly contains *the Words of God*. When studied in faith, our lives are forever changed for the better. We become wiser than ever.

As a young adult from a broken (and fatherless) home, God's Holy Spirit spoke to me in my heart. He said, "If you want wisdom, study the Bible." That made perfect sense to me because the Bible couldn't have survived (for hundreds of years) if it wasn't impacting lives.

Since the Bible is so remarkable, why is it so underappreciated in our society?

We've neglected the Bible because it's available and *free* to read at libraries or online. In addition, skeptics have criticized the Bible. Finally, believers who have been truly transformed by the Bible (like me) haven't been vocal enough.

You can bypass the stupid mistakes I made early in life.

Study the Bible in faith and reverence – then purpose in your heart to obey. Advice that sounds antiquated or commonplace now will stand out as "sage" later in life.

Yes, we can finish our first read of the entire Bible from Genesis to Revelation in a reasonable amount of time. If this is your goal, start with the audio version of the New Testament.

When I made up my mind to read the entire Bible in faith, I started with audio and finished the entire Bible in one month!

I accomplished this by listening as I cleaned the house, as I traveled, before going to sleep and at every opportunity. In life, we never *finish* reading the Bible. As we live, we reread passages and meditate on them for greater revelation.

Did you know that God promised to make us successful in every area of life if we meditate on His Biblical Word day and night?

This Book of the Law shall not depart from your mouth, but you shall meditate in it day and night, that you may observe to do according to all that is written in it. For then you will make your way prosperous, and then you will have good success (Joshua 1:8, NKJV).

Five

YOU HAVE NO COMPETITION IN LIFE.

This realization is huge. Competition is a false perception. Don't buy into it. You are different, and excellence always stands out. Don't compete; instead, habitually do your best. Make mastery and honor your trademarks and let them speak for you every day.

A man's gift makes room for him, And brings him before great men (Proverbs 18:16, NKJV).

We do not dare to classify or compare ourselves with some who commend themselves. When they measure themselves by themselves and compare themselves with themselves, they are not wise (2 Corinthians 10:12, NIV).

Six

GUARD YOUR HEART.

*T*here is no reason to ever have a broken heart. Spending time getting to know someone before committing to a relationship is key to avoiding heartbreak. We can learn how to accurately discern another's true intentions before becoming emotionally invested.

Discover who they *really* are. Our ability to exercise patience helps to avoid many disastrous situations. God *always* warns us! Look and listen. Never leap. The main reason for the failed relationships I've observed is that they moved too fast and ignored warning signs.

If anyone left you (spiritually), you no longer need them. God never leaves us without His strength and resources to succeed.

Marry a person who loves God and adores you!

You deserve to have honorable people in your life who have your best interests at heart.

Guard your heart above all else, for it determines the course of your life (Proverbs 4:23, NLT).

Seven

HEALING COMES WITH FORGIVENESS.

*E*liminate unnecessary stress by refusing to get offended and learning to forgive quickly. We must get over it or get help.

> **Genuine humility makes it easier to get along with others.**

Moreover, we should avoid being harsh or arrogant towards anyone, even children.

The Bible tells us, "Don't let the sun go down on your anger" (Ephesians 4:26). It is vital to learn from our mistakes, but we must not allow them to make us bitter and sick.

And be kind to one another, tenderhearted, forgiving one another, even as God in Christ forgave you (Ephesians 4:32, NKJV).

Eight

OUR BEAUTY RADIATES FROM WITHIN.

*G*od didn't create any junk! Genuine beauty emanates from within (1 Peter 3:4). Remember that a person who is kind, caring, and upbeat is beautiful to behold.

Don't be concerned about the outward beauty of fancy hairstyles, expensive jewelry, or beautiful clothes. You should clothe yourselves instead with the beauty that comes from within, the unfading beauty of a gentle and quiet spirit, which is so precious to God (1 Peter 3:3-4, NLT).

Nine

OUR GIFTS AND TALENTS SET US APART FROM EVERYONE ELSE.

*T*here is no other like you; you are unique, original (Romans 12:6). You cannot be replaced. You are just as impressive as anyone else on this planet.

> *In his grace, God has given us different gifts for doing certain things well. So if God has given you the ability to prophesy, speak out with as much faith as God has given you. If your gift is serving others, serve them well. If you are a teacher, teach well (Romans 12:6-7, NLT).*

Ten

WE HAVE ALWAYS BEEN (AND ALWAYS WILL BE) WORTHY OF LOVE AND RESPECT.

*S*how kindness and respect to everyone. Then, expect it to flow back to you. If someone else does not know how to show respect, that does not alter who you are. Show respect to even the most difficult individuals.

In good taste, we should avoid using profanity in everyday conversation. It remains offensive to many of our colleagues, and they may be too kind to complain.

Speaking of respect, it's wise to show respect to our children at any age. In doing so, it inspires them to respect us and others.

Respect everyone, and love the family of believers. Fear God, and respect the king (1 Peter 2:17, NLT).

Eleven

WE ARE NOT OUR PAST (OR OUR FAMILY'S PAST).

*I*n fact, your past no longer exists; your only concern is with the present. You can always start over. Each day is a new beginning and an opportunity to work towards a successful tomorrow.

Forget the former things; do not dwell on the past (Isaiah 43:18, NIV).

Twelve

DO WHAT YOU LOVE!

*I*n your career, do what you love. Wherever you are in life, share your true gifting. If you are not currently in your true calling, find a way to express that gift on an ongoing basis. It could be through tutoring, a hobby, taking classes, volunteering, or starting a part-time business. Never postpone or bury your dream. If you can't work in your purpose full-time, work on it part-time.

It is prudent to avoid all debt, then save and invest early in life. Lucrative investments have the ability to fuel our dreams. Success will require self-discipline and determination.

However, doing what we love makes time fly by; it restores our joy and has a reward within itself.

Whatever you do, work at it with all your heart, as working for the Lord, not for human masters, since you know that you will receive an inheritance from the Lord as a reward. It is the Lord Christ you are serving (Colossians 3:24, NIV).

Thirteen

GUARD YOUR MIND.

*D*istance yourself from influences that you know are detrimental, toxic, and negative. Do what is right, even if it goes against the opinions of others. Never back down from defending what is right, and don't feel the need to apologize for it.

> *Finally, brethren, whatever things are true, whatever things are noble, whatever things are just, whatever things are pure, whatever things are lovely, whatever things are of good report, if there is any virtue and if there is anything praiseworthy—meditate on these things (Philippians 4:8, NKJV).*

Fourteen

REFUSE TO BE BRAINWASHED.

*M*ost of what we see and hear is negative, not to mention false, like fake news. Learn to discern what is true from what is fake, both in real life and the media. Question everything.

Don't copy the behavior and customs of this world, but let God transform you into a new person by changing the way you think. Then you will learn to know God's will for you, which is good and pleasing and perfect (Romans 12:2, NLT).

Fifteen

BE GREAT BY
BEING YOURSELF.

*L*earn from humans, but don't copy them. Instead, be an individual in your own right. Try not to be offended when people reject you, don't like you, or don't understand you. It's not personal; we don't know what they've experienced or what they are currently suffering. As long as we are honorable and doing our best, what others think of us is none of our business. We can let it go.

Never let loyalty and kindness leave you!
Tie them around your neck as a reminder.
Write them deep within your heart.
Then you will find favor with both God
and people, and you will earn a good
reputation (Proverbs 3:3-4, NLT).

Sixteen

GOD IS OUR INNER COMPASS AND WE WILL ALWAYS BE TOLD WHAT TO DO!

*D*o the right thing always, and never compromise. We have no need to. When we compromise our higher values, it's *always* a trap, and we are detouring from God's highest plan for our lives.

> *Call to Me, and I will answer you, and show*
> *you great and mighty things, which you*
> *do not know (Jeremiah 33:3, NKJV).*

Seventeen

EXPECT A GREAT OUTCOME.

*W*e can accomplish what we set our minds to. We can excel in our field, regardless of statistics or the news.

Never give up. Remain creative and upbeat. We are not exactly like others who failed before us. Studying trends has some usefulness, but it shouldn't discourage us from trying alternate avenues that promise to be lucrative. Aim for the stars.

> *Ask and it will be given to you; seek and you will find; knock and the door will be opened to you. For everyone who asks receives; the one who seeks finds; and to the one who knocks, the door will be opened (Matthew 7:7-8, NIV).*

Eighteen

HONOR YOUR FATHER AND MOTHER.

*W*e don't honor our parents because we approve of their performance; we honor them because it is the right thing to do. Simple gestures like calling our parents, speaking to them kindly, and looking after them, have immeasurable worth.

Honoring our parents is the first commandment with a promise of blessing attached; we will live a long, good life as a reward (Exodus 20:12). We should never allow anyone to disrespect our parents. We shouldn't, our spouse shouldn't, nor our children.

Let's enthusiastically remember Mother's Day and Father's Day with a call, a greeting, or thoughtful gift.

Genuine humility is the key to harmonious relationships, whereas false pride and egotism lead to anger and division.

Unfortunately, some parents are emotionally broken and abusive. In these cases we must create healthy boundaries. We may need to live independently, and secure housing away from the parent. We have no obligation to allow unhealthy parents to manipulate us or be a bad example in front of our children.

It is challenging, but by living independently we can have a healthier relationship with emotionally ill parents. We can continue to love them unconditionally, do small kindnesses for them, remember holidays, and help them when we are able. It is never appropriate to talk to parents disrespectfully or allow resentment and unforgiveness to fill our hearts.

Keep parents in daily prayer and ask God for strength and wisdom to be a blessing to them.

Honor your father and mother. Then you will live a long, full life in the land the LORD your God is giving you (Exodus 20:12, NLT).

Nineteen

NOBODY
IS PERFECT.

*E*ach one of us must constantly improve to become a better version of ourselves. And, if we are not perfect ourselves, why do we make such unrealistic demands on others?

Create healthy boundaries to support harmony. Work to overcome feelings of anger, hatred, passing judgment, and discouragement. Negative emotions poison our souls and open a door for Satan to hurt us and others.

Love is patient and kind. Love is not jealous or boastful or proud or rude. It does not demand its own way. It is not irritable, and it keeps no record of being wronged (1 Corinthians 13:4-5, NLT).

Twenty

OUR MOST VALUABLE GOD-GIVEN GIFT IS FAITH.

*F*irst, have faith in God as a Being who loves us just as we are, is watching over us, and is committed to our success.

Second, have faith in yourself as a great individual who is needed in every space or arena that we find ourselves in. We showed up for a purpose in this world, and the world truly needs our contribution.

And whatever you ask in prayer, you will receive, if you have faith (Matthew 21:22, ESV).

Twenty-one

NEVER EVER WORRY – IT WON'T SOLVE ANYTHING.

*W*orry, blame, and criticism only make things worse, and they are a massive waste of time. They drain our energy and compromise our health.

Instead of worrying, practice gratitude.

Gratitude restores our joy and allows us to see challenges from a balanced perspective.

By training ourselves to stop worrying, we greatly enhance our physical and mental well-being while we are young.

Don't worry about anything; instead, pray about everything. Tell God what you need, and thank him for all he has done. Then you will experience God's peace, which exceeds anything we can understand. His peace will guard your hearts and minds as you live in Christ Jesus (Philippians 4:6-7, NLT).

UNDERSTAND THE MEANING OF LIFE

*I*n my life, I've known a few people who considered themselves wise and wealthy. However, at times I noticed troubling inconsistencies in their lives. Although people may be rich in material possessions, sometimes they are deficient in character. Due to their flawed value system, their family relationships often suffer.

As I read the Bible, a passage called "The Rich Fool" caught my attention, and I've meditated on the verses often. Our life priorities are critical.

It bears repeating that in life, the order of priority should be God, family, and career, respectively.

The absence of God's peace and family love has caused great suffering, which is truly heartbreaking.

We are not living in the earth realm by accident.

Every day we are confronted with the choice between good and evil, and we must resist the temptation to choose the latter. It may seem insignificant now, but the decisions we make on a daily basis will eventually lead us to our eternal destination. Moreover, making the right choices is essential for achieving success and fulfillment in life, as the wrong ones may lead to failure and hopelessness.

The patience of God is truly remarkable! He grants us enough time to seek Him, understand Him, and comply with His will.

Rather than focus on our sins, God has remained focused on His steadfast love for us.

By seeking God's wisdom, we can bypass avoidable errors and attract love and success throughout our lifetime.

Jesus Teaches
THE PARABLE OF THE RICH FOOL

Then He told them a parable: The ground of a certain rich man produced an abundance. So he thought to himself, "What shall I do, since I have nowhere to store my crops?" Then he said, "This is what I will do: I will tear down my barns and will build bigger ones, and there I will store up all my grain and my goods. Then I will say to myself, 'You have plenty of good things laid up for many years. Take it easy. Eat, drink, and be merry!'"

But God said to him, "You fool! This very night your life will be required of you. Then who will own what you have accumulated?"

This is how it will be for anyone who stores up treasure for himself but is not rich toward God.

—Luke 12:16-21, BSB

What is God saying? He is saying that we don't know the day and hour of our death. Therefore, it is foolhardy to ignore our spiritual life, even when things look their rosiest!

47

WHAT I BELIEVE ABOUT YOU

God made each of us in His likeness and image (Genesis 1:27). Therefore, we came to the earth realm with many of His own attributes and capabilities. In fact, Jesus said, "All things are possible to him who believes" (Mark 9:23, NKJV).

> **I know you have been positioned by God to succeed.**

1. I believe that you have enormous potential.
2. I believe that you can make a huge impact (for good) on the people in your current sphere of influence.

3. I believe that you will pass that exam, win that race, and excel in that job!

4. I believe that you will keep rising to the top wherever you work because of your great attitude, excellent work ethic, loyalty and integrity.

5. I believe that you can live a balanced life, including spiritual maturity, maintaining close family ties, a healthy diet, and exercise.

6. I believe that no matter where you start, you can migrate to doing what you love best if you remain determined to do so. Start small and grow gradually.

7. People fail because they don't *think* about life. Think deeply about why you are on this planet. Socrates said, "The unexamined life is not worth living."

8. I believe that you have the God-given wisdom and self-discipline to avoid the traps of worrying, harboring resentment against others, and neglecting the development of your spiritual and physical health.

9. I believe that you are, and will continue to be, a leader who isn't afraid to say what's right and do what's right, despite resistance from others.

10. I believe that if and when you choose to marry, you will be a great provider and an honorable role model for your family and children.
11. I believe that you can see the beauty in all people, and you will live in such a way that they can see the beauty within you.
12. I believe you can be the catalyst that inspires everyone in your extended family.

The LORD bless you and keep you; The LORD make His face shine upon you, And be gracious to you; The LORD lift up His countenance upon you, And give you peace (Numbers 6:24-26, NKJV).

THE SOURCE OF WISDOM

The Bible has earned the title of being the most popular book worldwide for a valid reason. Its teachings go back to the earliest days of humanity and offer us profound insights. Purchase the Holy Bible and study it with an open mind. Begin reading with a firm commitment to complete the entire book.

Both education and experience have value. However, wisdom is earned from meditating on the Word of God. The Bible comes in an audio version and is available free online.

For the LORD grants wisdom!
From his mouth come knowledge and
understanding (Proverbs 2:6, NLT).

LIVE A MORE MEANINGFUL LIFE

*M*y hope is that you will always be noble, full of faith, and determined to be that great and positive person you were created to be. Resist discouragement because you have already been equipped to make a positive difference in this world.

The smallest gestures can leave the biggest impact. It starts with one person ... YOU! Make the most significant choice of your life. Right now, dedicate or rededicate your life to Jesus. God's love for us is unconditional and He accepts us as we are. But without a connection with Him, we cannot attain our full potential.

> **A profound and supernatural transformation took place in my circumstances when I committed my life to God.**

I knew it was God. It was amazing!

For the LORD God is a sun and shield;
The LORD will give grace and glory;
No good thing will He withhold from those
who walk uprightly (Psalm 84:11, NKJV).

The following prayer transformed my life, and it has the power to change yours as well. Say this prayer in faith and be born-again in Christ. Then connect with a local Bible-based church and begin to study the Holy Bible daily.

PRAYER FOR SALVATION

"Father God, I come to you just as I am. You know how I've lived. I repent of all my sins. Forgive me. Lord Jesus, I believe you are the Son of God, and you died on the cross to forgive my sins. Come into my heart. Live your life in and through me from this day forward. Please fill me with your precious Holy Spirit. I belong to you, and I believe that I am saved!"

For this is how God loved the world:
He gave his one and only Son, so that

everyone who believes in him will not perish but have eternal life (John 3:16, NLT).

Give all your worries and cares to God, for he cares about you (1 Peter 5:7, NLT).

About the
AUTHOR

---

*G*ail **Marie King, MA,** is an author, speaker, and entrepreneur. She was called to ministry in 2009. She has earned a bachelor's degree in Counseling Psychology and a master's degree in Guidance and Counseling. Gail resides in Chicago, Illinois, with her loving family.

Crush Anxiety, Fear & Pain: Keys to Healing
Divine Healing: All Things Are Possible
Saving Relationships: Mastering Love and Peace
Marry A Man Who Loves God and Adores You
Is He The One: Be Guided by God In Love
In Hindsight: Words of Wisdom In Quotes
His Spoken Word: In Lyrics & Poetry
21 Insights I Wish Mom Taught Me

Gail King Website:
https://gailking.com/

Contact Gail:
https://gailking.com/contact/

Mentoring:
https://gailking.com/mentoring/

Speaking / Training Topics:
https://gailking.com/speaking/